MW00626290

The Christmas Story in Scripture

The Christmas Story in Scripture

With Paintings, Poems, and Prayers

CATHERINE M. AMENDOLIA

RESOURCE *Publications* · Eugene, Oregon

THE CHRISTMAS STORY IN SCRIPTURE
With Paintings, Poems, and Prayers

Resource Publications
An Imprint of Wipf and Stock Publishers
199 W. 8th Ave., Suite 3
Eugene, OR 97401

www.wipfandstock.com

PAPERBACK ISBN: 978-1-6667-7666-9
HARDCOVER ISBN: 978-1-6667-7667-6
EBOOK ISBN: 978-1-6667-7668-3

All scriptures New American Standard
Open Bible Edition
Thomas Nelson Publishers, 1979

To God be the glory

For Jim
Jean, James, Deana, John, Mary
and Barb
With special thanks to Jo

Table of Contents

Birth of John the Baptist Foretold

Luke 1:5–17

In the days of Herod, king of Judea, there was a priest named Zacharias, of the division of Abijah; and he had a wife from the daughters of Aaron, and her name was Elizabeth. They were both righteous in the sight of God, walking blamelessly in all the commandments and requirements of the Lord. And yet they had no child, because Elizabeth was infertile, and they were both advanced in years.

Now it happened that while he was performing his priestly service before God in the appointed order of his division, according to the custom of the priestly office, he was chosen by lot to enter the temple of the Lord and burn incense. And the whole multitude of the people were in prayer outside at the hour of the incense offering. Now an angel of the Lord appeared to him, standing to the right of the altar of incense. Zacharias was troubled when he saw the angel, and fear gripped him. But the angel said to him, "Do not be afraid, Zacharias, for your prayer has been heard, and your wife Elizabeth will bear you a son, and you shall name him John. You will have joy and gladness, and many will rejoice over his birth. For he will be great in the sight of the Lord; and he will drink no wine or liquor, and he will be filled with the Holy Spirit while still in his mother's womb. And he will turn many of the sons of Israel back to the Lord their God. And it is he who will go as a forerunner before Him in the spirit and power of Elijah, to turn the hearts of fathers back to their children, and the disobedient to the attitude of the righteous, to make ready a people prepared for the Lord."

Detail from The Annunciation
El Greco, 1576

Gabriel

That God would send His angel
To announce the marvelous plan
Of entrusting His Salvation
Into ordinary human hands
Confounds as sacred mystery
Beyond the human scope
But God does as He pleases
Leaving puzzled men to cope

For angels have the purpose
Of messaging the Lord's design
To unsuspecting persons
And dare they not decline
Despite disrupting human lives
Men accept their Maker's request
Seeking only to please the Master
Assured His methods ever best

In the years since Gabriel appeared
To those gentle, chosen folk
We still stand in awe and amazement
Of all those to whom he spoke
Angelic pronouncements from on high
Which seem incredible indeed
Yet mankind conforming to God's will
Is something all should heed

Dear God in whom all things are possible, you astonish us with both the natural and the supernatural! We stand in awe of who you are. You commanded the angel to appear on the earth at your bidding to deliver sacred messages and to announce your holy plans. You specifically chose Gabriel, your messenger angel, to speak to Zacharias and announce answered prayer for him and his wife, Elizabeth. You choose ordinary people for extraordinary ways to carry out your purposes. We are amazed at how you arrange things! You are a great and awesome God. You do exceedingly abundantly above all we could ever ask or think. Amen.

Zacharias' Reply

Luke 1:18–22

Zacharias said to the angel, "How will I know this? For I am an old man, and my wife is advanced in her years." The angel answered and said to him, "I am Gabriel, who stands in the presence of God, and I was sent to speak to you and to bring you this good news. And behold, you will be silent and unable to speak until the day when these things take place, because you did not believe my words, which will be fulfilled at their proper time."

And meanwhile the people were waiting for Zechariah, and were wondering at his delay in the temple. But when he came out, he was unable to speak to them; and they realized that he had seen a vision in the temple, and he repeatedly made signs to them, and remained speechless.

Archangel Gabriel Struck Dumb Zachariah
Alexander Ivanov, 1824

Zacharias

Here in the outer courts
We have waited ever so long
Where are you blameless Zacharias?
What on earth could have gone wrong?

We could not know in performing your duty
While standing beside the altar
That you encountered a holy angel
And your solid faith would then falter.

In secret did your sin take place
For you doubted your wife would conceive
It all happened in a hasty instant
When Gabriel you refused to believe.

Why do you seem so changed, so different
Since out of the temple you have come?
We could not have known what you replied
Would cause you to be struck dumb.

But you were appointed high priest for life
You are righteous, holy, and pious
Because you doubted you have been chastised
Now you can't speak, Zacharias.

It was promised that you would sire a son
A prayer answered with joyous relief
You have experienced God's love in action
Now Lord, help Thou our own unbelief.

Lord, thank you that you chastise those you love as you did Zacharias. At the time it probably seemed harsh to have his voice taken away, but this is what you chose for him. How else will we grow spiritually unless you chastise us as well? We know it is because you love us that you do these things. Help us to always be obedient when we receive direction from you, but please forgive us when we fail. We pray this in Jesus name. Amen.

The Birth of Jesus Foretold

Luke 1:26–38

Now in the sixth month the angel Gabriel was sent from God to a city in Galilee named Nazareth, to a virgin betrothed to a man whose name was Joseph, of the descendants of David; and the virgin's name was Mary. And coming in, he said to her, "Greetings, favored one! The Lord is with you." But she was very perplexed at this statement, and was pondering what kind of greeting this was. And the angel said to her, "Do not be afraid, Mary, for you have found favor with God. And behold, you will conceive in your womb and give birth to a son, and you shall name Him Jesus. He will be great and will be called the Son of the Most High; and the Lord God will give Him the throne of His father David; and He will reign over the house of Jacob forever, and His kingdom will have no end." But Mary said to the angel, "How will this be, since I am a virgin?" The angel answered and said to her, "The Holy Spirit will come upon you, and the power of the Most High will overshadow you; for that reason also the holy Child will be called the Son of God. And behold, even your relative Elizabeth herself has conceived a son in her old age, and she who was called infertile is now in her sixth month. For nothing will be impossible with God." And Mary said, "Behold, the Lord's bond-servant; may it be done to me according to your word." And the angel departed from her.

The Annunciation
Henry Ossawa Tanner, 1898

The Annunciation

*

Mary
Teenager
Handmaiden
Chosen by God
Betrothed to Joseph
Gentle and quiet spirit
Beheld the angel Gabriel
Greatly favored child of God
You will conceive and bear a Son
For all things are possible with God
He will be called Son of the Most High
He will have a Kingdom that knows no end
The Holy Spirit will come to overshadow you
Your body will host the dawn of the New Covenant
This is God's sovereign plan for the salvation of all men
Holy
Good
Love
Jesus

Father God, from the very beginning you knew the way of salvation for all. We praise you for sending your Holy Spirit and for Mary's willingness to give birth to the Son of God, the Prince of Peace. May we put our faith and trust in you even as Mary did. We are especially grateful that with you absolutely nothing is impossible. Help us never to doubt or question your ways, but to accept with grateful hearts what you have prepared for each of us from the foundation of the world. Please give us the faith to believe your mighty promises, for it is in your name we pray. Amen.

Mary Visits Elizabeth

Luke 1:39–45

Now at this time Mary set out and went in a hurry to the hill country, to a city of Judah, and she entered the house of Zacharias and greeted Elizabeth. When Elizabeth heard Mary's greeting, the baby leaped in her womb, and Elizabeth was filled with the Holy Spirit. And she cried out with a loud voice and said, "Blessed are you among women, and blessed is the fruit of your womb! And how has it happened to me that the mother of my Lord would come to me? For behold, when the sound of your greeting reached my ears, the baby leaped in my womb for joy. And blessed is she who believed that there would be a fulfillment of what had been spoken to her by the Lord."

Meeting of Mary and Elizabeth
Marx Reichlich, 1511

Mary's Joyful Visit

Elizabeth's heart sang at Mary's glad greeting
Oh, Spirit-filled moment of extraordinary meeting
For each woman well knew they would soon birth a boy
In unison their spirits skipped gleefully with joy

Then Mary's psalm burst forth in prophetic exclamation
Prayers ascending like myrrh, glorious declaration
Her spirit rejoicing, lauding God her Savior
In holy affirmation recounting His great favor

Remembering the fathers and prophets of old
Knowing all generations would henceforth be told
Of God's magnificent intent ever best
From now on all generations would call Mary blessed

Gentle and loving Lord Jesus, thank you for the joy of expectant hope; for family and for new life. We give you praise that you form and shape us in our mother's womb and we are fearfully and wonderfully made. We give you glory that you, the Son of Man, humbled yourself to become one of us. We praise you for this beautiful story of Elizabeth's great joy and Mary's remarkable conception. Both women rejoiced at their meeting. Young Mary yielded herself to your design for all of us; Elizabeth was too old to give birth, yet you did the impossible for both women. Please make us willing to be your instruments in whatever you choose to do in us. Amen.

Joseph's Encounter

Matthew 1:18–25

Now the birth of Jesus the Messiah was as follows: when His mother Mary had been betrothed to Joseph, before they came together she was found to be pregnant by the Holy Spirit. And her husband Joseph, since he was a righteous man and did not want to disgrace her, planned to send her away secretly. But when he had thought this over, behold, an angel of the Lord appeared to him in a dream, saying, "Joseph, son of David, do not be afraid to take Mary as your wife; for the Child who has been conceived in her is of the Holy Spirit. She will give birth to a Son; and you shall name Him Jesus, for He will save His people from their sins." Now all this took place so that what was spoken by the Lord through the prophet would be fulfilled: "Behold, the virgin will conceive and give birth to a Son, and they shall name Him Immanuel," which translated means, "God with us." And Joseph awoke from his sleep and did as the angel of the Lord commanded him, and took Mary as his wife, and kept her a virgin until she gave birth to a Son; and he called His name Jesus.

Saint Joseph
James Tissot, 1886 - 1894

Joseph

What manner of man this Joseph
Who amidst planed shingles and sawdust floor
(Where cedar scent of carpentry arose)
Sought only quiet anonymity, nothing more?

Noble Joseph of David's line
Wishing merely to spare his betrothed shame
Seeking a righteous solution
In integrity he assigned her no blame

Gentle Joseph by loyalty bound
But her condition he could not endorse
So wracked by conflicting emotions
Reluctantly opted for quiet divorce

Slumber Joseph in heavenly sleep
Laboriously lost in prophetic dream
Awed by the angelic instructions
Now compliant with God's sovereign scheme

Husband and surrogate father
Neither esteemed nor honored in men's eyes
But God has chosen the world's weak
Men like this Joseph to confound the wise

Jesus, you grew up as a carpenter's son. Joseph, your surrogate father, taught you his trade. He was a steadfast man. Thank you, Lord, for men of integrity like Joseph; humble men who work quietly at their occupation, all the while careful to heed your voice in obedience. Father, please cause men today to follow Joseph's example by leading quiet, godly lives. Whether professional men, or those who labor in other ways, may they be men after your own heart. We pray this in Jesus holy name. Amen.

Jesus' Birth in Bethlehem

Luke 2:1–7

Now in those days a decree went out from Caesar Augustus, that a census be taken of all the inhabited earth. This was the first census taken while Quirinius was governor of Syria. And all the people were on their way to register for the census, each to his own city. Now Joseph also went up from Galilee, from the city of Nazareth, to Judea, to the city of David which is called Bethlehem, because he was of the house and family of David, in order to register along with Mary, who was betrothed to him, and was pregnant. While they were there, the time came for her to give birth. And she gave birth to her firstborn son; and she wrapped Him in cloths, and laid Him in a manger, because there was no room for them in the inn.

Nativity
Gari Melchers, 1891
Gari Melchers Home and Studio – Gari Melchers

Mary's Plight

Harsh the coming cold evening air
And she heavy with child that long-ago night
Wearily jostled along atop the plodding donkey
Each step more taxing – such misery to bear

Harsh her disappointment but harsher still
The sting of rejection from the words, "no room"
While she longed for her home, its warmth
Yet this could not be by her own will

Harsh the pains she panted, labored strong;
Strained to give birth with prickly straw beneath her
In the grimy stable full of strange smells with
Just a whisper of wind – lone quiet song

Harsh His cry that pierced the dark: the Babe was born!
Close she nestled Him, so tiny, so helpless He
She wondered what His future held, this Child of Promise,
Messiah! A mystery! And she perplexed, forlorn

Harsh reality dawned with the newness of day
That hereafter she must live by persistent faith
And the voice of the angel still echoed strong
As Jesus peacefully in the manger lay

Jesus, you are the Incarnation, the Christ, the Anointed of God who came amongst us in human form, born as a helpless baby. You are the Mighty God. Thank you that you modeled humility to us by your humble birth in a stable. We read in the Scripture of the great rejoicing at your birth and not of any grumbling at the hardship surrounding it! We acknowledge that your ways often seem strange to us, and that they are sometimes difficult both to understand and to live out; nevertheless, may we live lives filled with awe and worship of who you are. In your name we pray. Amen.

Angels Announce Jesus Birth

Luke 2:8–14

In the same region there were some shepherds staying out in the fields and keeping watch over their flock at night. And an angel of the Lord suddenly stood near them, and the glory of the Lord shone around them; and they were terribly frightened. And so the angel said to them, "Do not be afraid; for behold, I bring you good news of great joy which will be for all the people; for today in the city of David there has been born for you a Savior, who is Christ the Lord. And this will be a sign for you: you will find a baby wrapped in cloths and lying in a manger." And suddenly there appeared with the angel a multitude of the heavenly army of angels praising God and saying, "Glory to God in the highest, And on earth peace among people with whom He is pleased."

The Annunciation to the Shepherds
Adam Pynacker, 1640

The Night Angels Sang

Came history's bright moment which long lay concealed
When at last the fullness of time was revealed
To lowly shepherds who on dark fields assembled
There appeared a lone angel, while fearfully they trembled
To these same shepherds where they lay encamped
'Round about them fair angel's radiance lamped
Heralding great news of Messiah's birth
Announcing wondrous tidings to those upon earth
Sudden glorious light when night's curtain parted!
With shimmering entrance angelic beings started
Resonating a chorus with voices blending
In perfect harmony of praise ascending
To the Father rapturous congratulations
Then earthward flew blissful incantations
Euphoric and splendid the celestial rejoicing
Toward all of creation their "gloria's" voicing
"Peace on earth to men of good will"
"Halleluiah! Halleluiah!" Echoed across hills
Mighty army of praising, a thunderous roar
From knighthood of angels, valiant wagers of war!
Against tenor refrains their "hosannas" blazing
Mixed soprano high notes – marvelous, amazing
The seraph choir with sweet glee resounding
Reverberated a jubilant concert abounding
Proclaimed they the Christ, promised made-flesh Word
To ordinary shepherds keeping watch over their herd
From this heavenly entourage glad worship rang
O! Majestic the anthem, the night angels sang!

Awesome Father, God of heaven and earth, how glorious that the angels rejoiced the night when Jesus was born! We can only imagine the jubilant singing! It was so incredibly gracious of you to allow the lowly shepherds to witness such a supernatural scene. What a celebration there must have been in heaven! May our hearts always be full of joy, praise, worship and thanksgiving to you. Thank you that you allowed everyday people like the shepherds to see what others over the centuries have only imagined. We join with the heavenly host to praise you, exalt you, and give you glory for humbly coming into the world as one of us. Amen.

Shepherds and Kings

Luke 2:15–18

When the angels had departed from them into heaven, the shepherds began saying to one another, "Let's go straight to Bethlehem, then, and see this thing that has happened which the Lord has made known to us." And they came in a hurry and found their way to Mary and Joseph, and the baby as He lay in the manger. When they had seen Him, they made known the statement which had been told them about this Child. And all who heard it were amazed about the things which were told them by the shepherds.

Matthew 2:1 and 2:9–11

Now after Jesus was born in Bethlehem of Judea in the days of Herod the king, behold, magi from the east arrived in Jerusalem, saying, "Where is He who has been born King of the Jews? For we saw His star in the east and have come to worship Him."

After hearing the king, [Herod] they went on their way; and behold, the star, which they had seen in the east, went on ahead of them until it came to a stop over the place where the Child was to be found. When they saw the star, they rejoiced exceedingly with great joy. And after they came into the house, they saw the Child with His mother Mary; and they fell down and worshiped Him. Then they opened their treasures and presented to Him gifts of gold, frankincense, and myrrh.

Journey of the Magi
James Tissot, 1894

Shepherds and Kings

Shepherds came, poor herdsmen, flocks in tow
Across rolling hills swiftly walking
While eagerly eyeing bright star's light
Of this night's wondrous events talking

Then came magi, wise men, learned kings
On camels, traipsing over desert sand
From far away East they journeyed long
Traveling on to Bethlehem's land

Draw near you shepherds, come close you kings
Come trembling to dusty stable's door
For as many who come are welcome here
Grand Hope-gates flung wide forevermore

For He will arise and shepherd His flock
The Great Shepherd and the King of all Kings
The infant Jesus, destined for the cross
Worship Him who our salvation brings

Jesus, you are our Good Shepherd and the King of Kings. No matter if our journey to you is short or long; no matter if we are poor or rich; if we hold a high place in society or a lowly one – you love us and welcome us to come to you to receive your salvation which is so very rich and free. May we gift you with how we conduct our lives. We worship you for who you are and for your love and your provision for all mankind no matter our earthly status. Amen.

The Word Made Flesh

John 1:14

And the Word became flesh, and dwelt among us; and we saw His glory, glory as of the only Son from the Father, full of grace and truth.

The Voyage of Life Old Age
Thomas Cole 1842

The Word Made Flesh

The darkness split allowing Light
God spoke radiance into sight
In Him was Life, the light of men
The Word made flesh precisely when
Full of truth and grace among us He dwelt
The promised Christ, now His presence now felt
For all creation to see His glory
Light of the world, eternal story

Creator God, Lord of the Universe, your timing is absolutely perfect. You spoke and it came to be. You sent Jesus at just the precise and perfect time in history. You promised a Savior for us way back in the beginning when Adam and Eve sinned, and you fulfilled what you said you would do when you sent Jesus. All your promises are yes and amen. You are trustworthy. We can rely on you. You send your Spirit to lead and guide us. Praise you for your faithfulness. Amen.

Jesus is Presented in the Temple

Luke 2:21–35

And when eight days were completed so that it was time for His circumcision, He was named Jesus, the name given by the angel before He was conceived in the womb. And when the days for their purification according to the Law of Moses were completed, they brought Him up to Jerusalem to present Him to the Lord (as it is written in the Law of the Lord: "Every firstborn male that opens the womb shall be called holy to the Lord"), and to offer a sacrifice according to what has been stated in the Law of the Lord: "A pair of turtledoves or two young doves." And there was a man in Jerusalem whose name was Simeon; and this man was righteous and devout, looking forward to the consolation of Israel; and the Holy Spirit was upon him. And it had been revealed to him by the Holy Spirit that he would not see death before he had seen the Lord's Christ. And he came by the Spirit into the temple; and when the parents brought in the child Jesus, to carry out for Him the custom of the Law, then he took Him in his arms, and blessed God, and said, "Now, Lord, You are letting Your bond-servant depart in peace, according to Your word; for my eyes have seen Your salvation, which You have prepared in the presence of all the peoples: a light for revelation for the Gentiles, and the glory of Your people Israel." And His father and mother were amazed at the things which were being said about Him. And Simeon blessed them and said to His mother Mary, "Behold, this Child is appointed for the fall and rise of many in Israel, and as a sign to be opposed—and a sword will pierce your own soul—to the end that thoughts from many hearts may be revealed.

Simeon in the Temple
Rembrandt, 1669

In the Temple

With gnarled hands and back no longer straight
Weathered face, and labored, lopsided gait,
To the temple, compelled, he hurries to seek
Father, mother, and baby: poor humble and meek.

Standing near as they offer the required sacrifice
Carefully he lifts the Baby – just this once will suffice.
As he gazes into Jesus' peaceful face
Swaddled Bundle he gently hugs in embrace.

On tired old bones rests his very salvation
And that of every tongue and tribe and nation.
He beholds the Ancient Promise fulfilled
Holy Innocent who must one day be killed.

And for this moment did he pray, hope and believe
By the Holy Spirit this longing he dared conceive –
Simeon, prophet of God, holy and devout
Prophesy's over Mary, with a confident shout:

"Behold many in Israel will rise and fall
Because this Child shall be a sign for all
And a sword your own heart will surely tear
While the thoughts of many shall be laid bare."

Jesus, it is such a tender and touching sight to see an old man gently cradling a baby. Thank you that no matter how long we live, even if we live to a very old age, you still want to use us for your kingdom purposes just as you used Simeon to prophesy over Jesus and his mother. Let us never think we should retire from your service; instead, even as our earthly bodies wear out, let us serve you gladly all the days of our lives. May our eyes, ears, feet, hands and hearts be ever willing to be of use to you. No matter what we hear you telling us to do, even if it's a very small thing, grant us, we pray, the grace to obey you. And please grant us a peaceful death as you granted your servant Simeon. Amen.

Anna

Luke 2:36–38

And there was a prophetess, Anna, the daughter of Phanuel, of the tribe of Asher. She was advanced in years and had lived with her husband for seven years after her marriage, and then as a widow to the age of eighty-four. She did not leave the temple grounds, serving night and day with fastings and prayers. And at that very moment she came up and began giving thanks to God, and continued to speak about Him to all those who were looking forward to the redemption of Jerusalem.

Simeon and Anna in the Temple
Rembrandt, 1627

Anna

A ragged shawl covered her hair of white
And stooped at the shoulder, her figure slight
Aged Anna curiously turned around
Eyes searching for whence came the sound
Of Simeon's booming voice declaring
Words of prophesy, while others began staring
As quickly she walked to the parent's side
Knowing this moment God did provide
Prophetess Anna, whose name means grace
Tenderly beheld Jesus' infant face
Emboldened by years of prayer and fasting
And putting her trust in God everlasting
She announced in the temple to all who came near
Of the salvation to come, with no reason to fear
Offering to God thanksgiving and praise
Fearlessly she spoke with clear voice raised
Giving glory to God, she spoke of Him
To those seeking redemption in Jerusalem

God of the aged, thank you for the beautiful story of Anna. The devotion she demonstrated by her steadfast years of prayer and fulfilling the spiritual discipline of fasting, despite her advanced age, is an inspiration to all, especially the elderly. May we learn from her example. May we not cease to practice the disciplines of praying and especially of fasting. May we be ever faithful to act when we hear you urging us to share your goodness with others. May you always receive the glory. Amen.

The Escape to Egypt

Matthew 2:13–15

Now when they had gone, behold, an angel of the Lord appeared to Joseph in a dream and said, "Get up! Take the Child and His mother and flee to Egypt, and stay there until I tell you; for Herod is going to search for the Child to kill Him." So Joseph got up and took the Child and his mother while it was still night, and left for Egypt. He stayed there until the death of Herod; this happened so that what had been spoken by the Lord through the prophet would be fulfilled: "Out of Egypt I called My Son."

Flight into Egypt
Eugene Giradet, 19th Century

Joseph's Second Dream

Arise, Joseph
Take the Child and flee
Flee with Mary
Go, you three

Flee Herod's men
Leave in haste; take flight
Heed this warning
Flee by night

Arise, Joseph
Take the Child and flee
Flee the danger
Go be free

Flee to Egypt
For their protection
Flee with speed
Await direction

Loving and caring Father, Joseph's willingness to hear and obey, even though it meant much disruption and inconvenience for his family is an inspiration to us. Surely his fleeing meant hardship for his family. When we suffer hardships, loss, disruptions and inconveniences to our daily lives, please remind us to be grateful and uncomplaining. We pray that you will fill us with your joy when we are forced to encounter changes to our lives. Make us willing to journey through this life with steadfast determination to serve you gratefully all of our days. We pray this in Jesus name. Amen.

Printed in the USA
CPSIA information can be obtained
at www.ICGtesting.com
LVHW060923290923
759640LV00005B/8

9 781666 776670